Story of Britain

2. BRITAIN IN THE MIDDLE AGES

Philip Sauvain

Illustrated by John Lobban

Nelson

Acknowledgements

The author and publishers wish to acknowledge the following photograph sources.

Mansell Collection pp. 6, 15, and 27.

Radio Times Hulton Picture Library p. 7.

The remainder of the photographs in this book were provided by the author.

The publishers have made every effort to trace the copyright holders, but if they have inadvertently overlooked any, they will be pleased to make the necessary arrangements at the first opportunity.

First published by Macmillan Education Ltd 1980

ISBN 0-333-27224-7

This edition published by Thomas Nelson & Sons Ltd 1991
ISBN 0-17-425062-2
NPN 9 8 7 6 5 4 3

Printed in China.

CONTENTS

1. WILLIAM THE CONQUEROR

It was a bad start. Only a few minutes after landing in England, Duke William had fallen flat on his face. The Norman soldiers were afraid this was a bad sign. They thought it meant that their Duke would be killed fighting the Saxons. But William quickly recovered. He held up a handful of earth and shouted: "Look! I have taken England already."

It was the year 1066. The Saxons had elected an earl called Harold as their king. But some years before, Harold had gone to France and had agreed that William should be the next king. Now William and the Normans had come to England to make Harold keep his promise.

William had sailed with about 7000 soldiers from Normandy (a place in France). They landed on a beach in Sussex. On 14 October they fought a great battle with King Harold and the Saxon army.

It started at 9.00 in the morning. The Saxon soldiers stood on top of a low hill. They held their shields so close together it was like a long wall. The Saxons fought with spears, swords and heavy battleaxes. The Normans fought with spears, swords and bows and arrows.

William the Conqueror landing at Pevensey

The Battle of Hastings

The battle began when the Norman archers fired their arrows at the Saxons. Then the Norman knights charged on horseback, but many of them were killed. The others turned and went back down the hill. Some of the Saxons thought they had won and ran after the Normans. But now they did not have a long wall of shields to protect them. They were easily cut down by the Norman knights.

Several times during the day the Normans attacked but could not make the rest of the Saxons give in. Then William tried another plan. He told his archers to fire their arrows high into the air. As the arrows showered down the Norman knights charged up the hill yet again. The Saxons were horrified to see Harold fall. The bravest Saxons still tried to fight on but most of them ran away. Duke William had won.

Scenes from the Bayeux Tapestry

We know a lot about the Norman Conquest and the battle of Hastings from a wonderful set of pictures called the Bayeux Tapestry. The pictures were stitched in coloured thread on to a long sheet of cloth. The whole story of the Norman Conquest is told in pictures. It is just like the way a comic tells a story today.

The pictures show the Normans getting their warships ready. Soldiers are loading weapons, armour and horses on to the boats. Then we see the Norman ships crossing the sea. The Normans land near Hastings. Pictures show the Norman soldiers in their camp. Then they show them going forward to meet the Saxons with archers in front and knights on horseback behind. The Saxon soldiers can be easily picked out because they were the only ones to fight with battleaxes.

Pictures of the battle show the Saxon soldiers standing close together holding their shields to make a wall. Horses and soldiers are shown falling and lying on the ground. Arrows and spears can be seen flying through the air.

Finally we see King Harold chopped down with a sword and the last of the Saxons running away.

Some Things To Do

The four pictures on these pages show scenes from the Bayeux Tapestry. Look at the pictures.

1. Which picture shows the Saxon soldiers standing with their shields close together?

2. Which picture shows the Norman archers?

3. How do we know that the Norman knights brought their own horses with them?

4. The picture of the death of Harold shows a man falling, struck down by a sword. The people who made the tapestry stitched the words "Harold Rex" (meaning King Harold) close by. Which picture shows this?

5. Copy the pictures of the Bayeux Tapestry. Write a few words under each of your pictures to say what is happening.

Afterwards

William was crowned King of England on Christmas Day 1066. Not all the Saxons agreed to obey William as their king. Saxons in the north of England fought against the Normans and captured the city of York. A Saxon nobleman called Hereward the Wake fought against the Normans in East Anglia.

William the Conqueror put down both of these rebellions. Many Saxons were killed and the Normans set fire to their houses and villages.

William also built a great castle, the Tower of London, to show the people of London how powerful he was. Many other castles were built in England by the Norman barons and knights, who had been given land by William in return for fighting for him.

2. LIVING IN A CASTLE

The wooden drawbridge rattled as the last of the knights rode hastily across. There was a creaking of chains as the bridge was lifted. The portcullis, a heavy wooden gate with spikes on the end, slammed down.

At last the people in the castle felt safe. A deep ditch filled with water (the moat) surrounded the thick walls of the castle. This would help to keep the enemy out.

Lookouts were sent up to the top of the castle tower. The archers stood behind narrow windows in the walls, ready to fire arrows at the enemy soldiers if they got too close. Other soldiers sheltered behind the low walls of stone at the tops of the walls and towers.

The portcullis

There were small gaps in the walls, or battlements, which made it easy for them to aim their arrows at the enemy. Sometimes they poured boiling oil or water on to the enemy soldiers below.

An enemy attacking a castle also had a number of tricks to play. They could hurl stones into the castle with machines rather like catapults.

At night they filled in the moat with mud and branches. Then they crossed over and tried to knock down the main gates with a battering ram. The enemy soldiers also built wooden towers and ladders as high as the walls. They pushed these up against the battlements so that their soldiers could try to climb over the castle walls.

When a castle was completely surrounded it was said to be under siege. If the siege lasted a long time the people inside might starve, so they stored large amounts of food inside the castle in case they were attacked. They also made sure that there was a well inside the castle walls so they would have fresh water.

A castle under siege

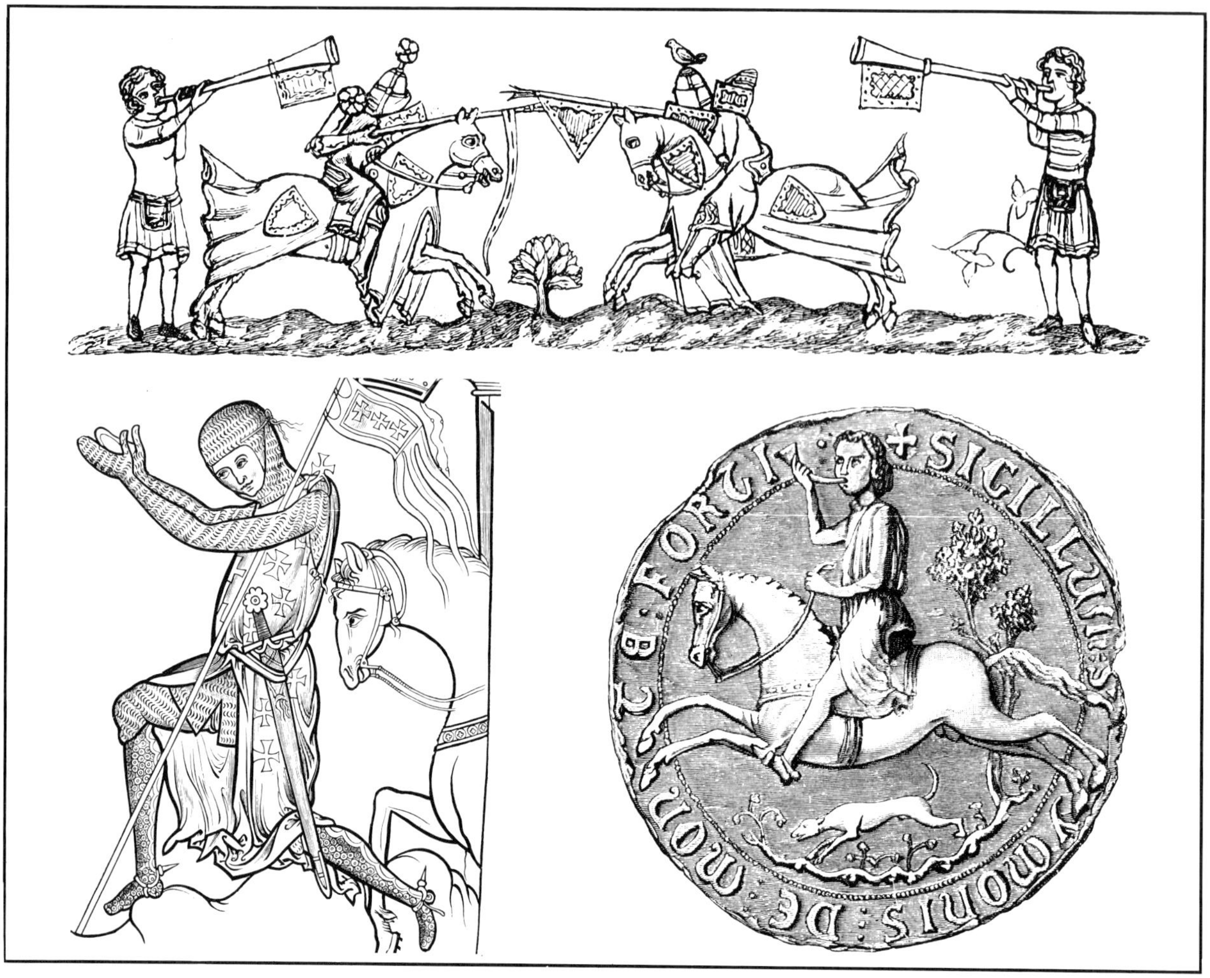

Life in Norman times

Old pictures show knights fighting each other on horseback in tournaments, hunting scenes and people eating in the Great Hall. The knights hunted deer, wild pigs, wolves and other animals. At the tournaments knights on horseback charged at each other each carrying a long spear called a lance. Although they carried shields and wore armour many knights were killed or injured in tournaments.

The baron and the knights, soldiers and servants all had their dinner together in the Great Hall of the castle. This was a long high room with the lord's table raised above the others at one end.

There was usually a huge log fire in the Hall. It was so hot that a whole sheep or pig could be put on a spike in front of it and roasted.

The baron's wife had a private room to sit in. This was called the solar. It was here that the children played with their toys and pets.

Some Things To Do

1. Look at the picture on page 9. Write a few words to say what is happening in it.

2. Draw a picture to show a tournament. Show two knights charging at each other carrying lances.

3. Look at the photograph at the bottom of page 8. Make a model of a portcullis from a piece of card. Draw the outline in pencil and then cut it out with scissors.

4. What scene in a castle is shown in the picture below? Copy this picture. Write a few words to say what is happening.

5. Write down two ways of trying to get into a castle which is under siege. Write down two ways of trying to stop the enemy soldiers attacking a castle.

Afterwards

When the English went to war in Wales about two hundred years after the battle of Hastings they built a number of new castles there. These castles at Caernarvon, Harlech, Conway and other places were very strong indeed.

When England became more peaceful it was not so necessary for a baron to live in a castle with thick walls and a moat. Rich people wanted to live in more comfort. Castles gradually began to look more like homes.

Dinner in the Great Hall

3. THE MURDER OF THOMAS BECKET

King Henry II was very angry with his former friend Thomas Becket, the Archbishop of Canterbury. He turned to the men near him and shouted at them in a temper: "Are you all cowards? Will no one rid me of this miserable priest?"

Four of his knights heard these words and quickly left for the city of Canterbury. They were called Reginald FitzUrse, William de Tracy, Hugh de Morville and Richard the Breton. They took a band of armed soldiers with them.

Canterbury Cathedral

At about 3.00 on the afternoon of 29 December 1170 they galloped into the courtyard of Canterbury Cathedral. Monks and priests ran from them in terror.

Other monks dragged the Archbishop to safety inside the Cathedral. When they were inside they tried to bolt the door, but Becket stopped them. "This is not a castle," he said. "Leave the door open."

Then the four knights strode into the Cathedral with sharp swords in their hands.

"Where is Thomas Becket, traitor to the King?" shouted Reginald FitzUrse.

"I am here," replied Becket. "No traitor to the King but a priest. I am surprised you come into church in such clothes. What do you want with me?"

The knights rushed forward and struck at Becket with their swords. After they had killed him Hugh de Morville shouted triumphantly, "Let's be on our way, knights. He'll rise no more."

As they left the Cathedral there was a flash of lightning and a crash of thunder.

The knights forcing their way into Canterbury Cathedral

Thomas Becket and Henry II had been friends but had quarrelled. Henry thought that the Archbishop of Canterbury and all the other priests should obey the King's laws. In those days bishops, abbots and many priests were very rich and powerful. They had been allowed many privileges before. They did not want to give up these rights to the King. Becket told Henry that he only obeyed God's laws.

The murder of Thomas Becket

When Henry learnt that Becket was dead he was very sorry. He walked through the streets of Canterbury in his bare feet and allowed himself to be whipped by the monks as punishment.

Three years later Thomas Becket was made a saint. People from all over Britain and Europe came to worship at the spot in the Cathedral where the murder had taken place. People who travel a long way specially to visit a holy place are called pilgrims.

Some Things To Do

1. Who killed Thomas Becket?

2. What is a pilgrim?

3. What do you think the people in the Cathedral thought when they heard the sound of thunder and saw the flash of lightning shortly after the death of their Archbishop?

4. The pictures on the opposite page show the murder of Becket. They were drawn by monks not very long after Becket's death. Are the two pictures the same? Which do you think is the better picture?

Afterwards

Every year pilgrims made the journey to Canterbury. Sick people hoped to get better by visiting the place where the Saint died.

In those days it took a long time to get from London to Canterbury. A man called Geoffrey Chaucer wrote some stories which might have been told by pilgrims to make the journey go more quickly. He called his book of stories *The Canterbury Tales*. It is one of the most famous books ever written in Britain.

Canterbury pilgrims in 1200

4. A KNIGHT AT THE CRUSADES

Not long after the murder of Thomas Becket the people of Europe heard terrible news. Crusaders in the Holy Land had been beaten in battle.

The Crusaders were Christian knights and soldiers from all over Europe who fought against the Moslems (or Saracens). Palestine was the Holy Land for the Christians but the Moslems wanted it as well. It was their land too.

The Crusaders had been beaten by a great Moslem leader called Saladin who had captured the Holy City of Jerusalem.

King Richard I of England wanted to join the other Crusaders. In December 1189 he sailed for Palestine with an army of knights and soldiers. After many adventures he reached the Holy Land in May 1191.

The Crusaders setting out for the Holy Land

A battle between Christians and Saracens

Richard landed near a city called Acre. For two years the Saracens had defended this city against the Crusaders who were already in the Holy Land. Now Richard took charge. He was so brave in battle people called him the Lionheart. When Richard I attacked Acre he used huge catapults to throw stones into the city. One man wrote: "A stone sent from one of them killed twelve men." Another writer said: "Day and night they battered the walls of the city."

It was not long before Acre surrendered. Although Richard was a good leader he could be very cruel. When Saladin captured Jerusalem he treated the Christian prisoners with kindness. But when Richard captured over 2000 Moslems at Acre he had them all put to death.

Something else happened at Acre. The Duke of Austria claimed that he should be equal in importance to the kings of England and France and raised his flag beside theirs. Later, he was furious to see that his flag had been torn down. He blamed Richard for this insult, and hated him very much.

Richard led the Crusaders towards Jerusalem. He defeated Saladin in a battle at a place called Arsuf.

Richard and Saladin admired each other. During the battle Saladin heard that Richard had lost his horse and was fighting on foot. Even though Richard was his enemy he sent a servant with two fine horses to replace those Richard had lost.

Some time later Richard got news of troubles at home in England and in Normandy. He knew he could not go on to capture Jerusalem now. Instead Saladin agreed to let Christian pilgrims visit Jerusalem.

Richard then sailed for home but was shipwrecked. Unfortunately he had to travel through the lands of the Duke of Austria. Although he was in disguise he was captured and thrown into prison. In the end the people of Britain had to pay a large sum of money (a ransom) to get their king back.

Richard I meeting Saladin in battle

Some Things To Do

1. Look at the picture on page 16. What did the Crusaders' ships look like? Draw a picture of one of their ships and write a few words underneath to say what it shows.

2. Pretend you are Richard I in prison. Write a letter to a friend telling the story of your adventures in the Holy Land and why you are now in prison.

3. Why did the Crusaders fight the Saracens?

4. Make a model of a Crusader's shield. Take a piece of thin cardboard and draw the shape of the shield on it in pencil. Paint a red cross on your shield. Cut the shield out with a pair of scissors. Cut out a piece of card and glue it to the back of the shield. Now you can stand your Crusader's shield up.

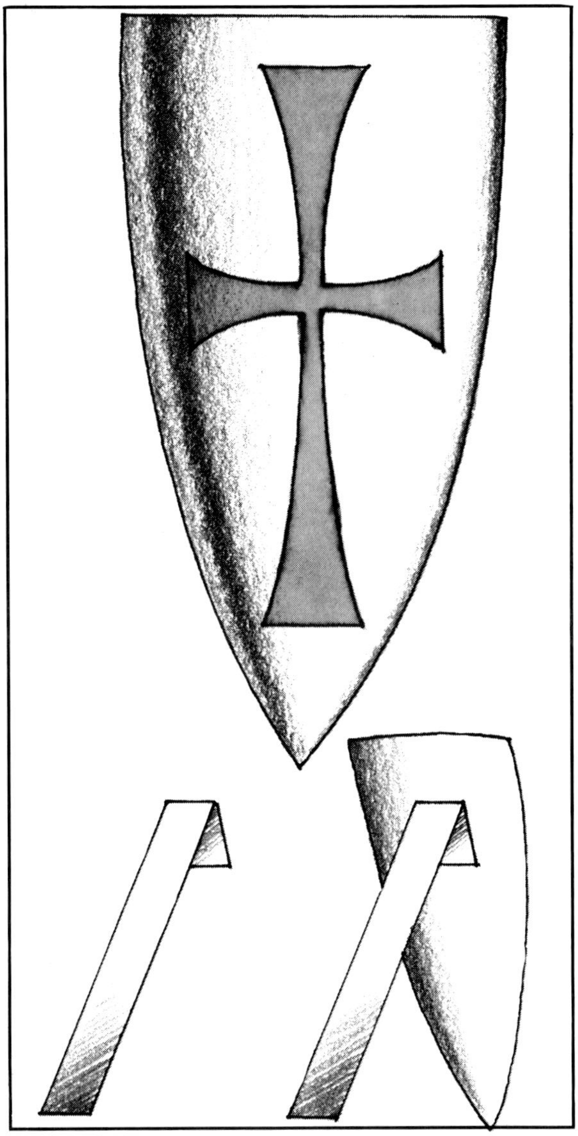

How to make a Crusader's shield

Afterwards

Some good things did come about as a result of the Crusades. The Crusaders brought back carpets, spices, cotton cloth and even monkeys and parrots. The cotton was called muslin after a place in the Middle East where it was made.

There were other Crusades to the Holy Land. About forty years after the time of Richard the Lionheart the Moslems agreed to give Jerusalem back to the Christians. But in 1244 it was captured again by the Moslems.

The Crusaders were never again to live in the Holy City of Jerusalem.

A village in medieval times

5. LIFE IN A MEDIEVAL VILLAGE

Hugh Free had let his cow stray into the lord's garden. He had to pay a sum of money as a fine. William Jordan was also fined for the poor job he had done when ploughing the lord's fields.

Both men lived in a village in Wiltshire about 750 years ago. We know this because the story of what happened then was written down in a book.

At that time most people in Britain were peasants like Hugh and William. They lived in a village owned by the lord of the manor. The lord of the manor was sometimes a baron, sometimes a knight and sometimes an abbot or prior in a monastery.

The huts in the village were built in the centre, close to the village green and the church. The lord's castle or manor house was some distance away.

The peasants' huts were made of wood and had thatched roofs. There was an open fire in the middle of the main room and sometimes a hole in the roof to let the smoke out. This made the walls of the hut very sooty.

There were only a few bits of furniture inside the hut, such as a wooden chest, a tub, a table and some stools. There was straw on the dirt floor. There were no windows so it was always dark and gloomy inside the hut.

The peasants ate very simple meals. Their vegetables came from their gardens, the milk from their cows, the bread from their corn and they brewed beer from their barley. If they had bacon it was from their own pigs.

A peasant's hut

The land in the village was usually divided into three large fields. Each year one of these fields grew wheat and a second grew barley or oats. The third field was given a rest from growing crops. The next year the order was changed. The third field grew wheat, the first field grew barley or oats and the second field had a rest.

These fields were divided into long strips of land. Each peasant had strips of land in each of the three fields. A peasant might have four strips in one field, three strips in another field, and five strips in the third. There was also a common where they could graze their cattle and sheep. They took their pigs to the woods to feed on acorns.

By the side of the river there was grassland (the meadow) where peasants could grow grass to feed their cattle in winter.

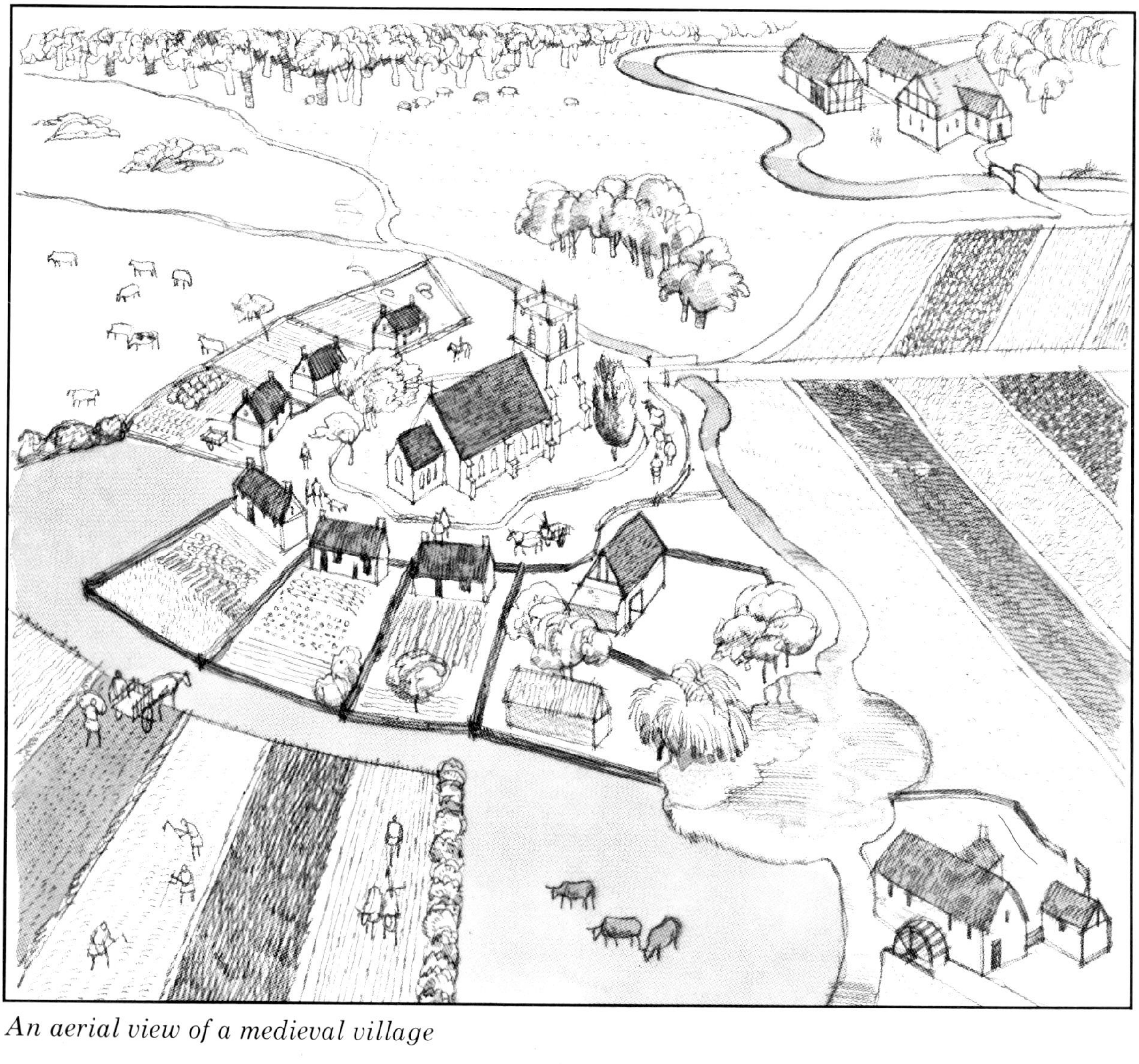

An aerial view of a medieval village

Life in a medieval village

In those days the peasants had to do a lot of work without pay for the lord of the manor. It was the rent they paid for the land they had been given.

We know what some of these jobs were because they were written down. In a village in Sussex a woman called Alice had to plough the lord's fields and had to carry firewood, manure, corn and hay in her cart. She also helped at harvest time. In another village in Sussex, William Orgon had to pay his lord a sum of money and also half a pig and two hens. He worked three days a week on the lord's land. He ploughed the fields, sowed seed, spread manure, dug ditches, hoed the ground and cut the corn.

For the rest of their time the peasants could work on their own strips of land. They worked all day from sunrise to sunset. It was a hard life. They often worked on Sundays. Only a few children went to school.

Most of the peasants had to live in the same village all their life. They were not free to do what they liked. They had to ask permission from their lord just to get married.

When they broke a law they were brought before the lord in the manor court and punished. Sometimes they were whipped or made to sit in the village stocks. This was a wooden board with holes for the wrongdoer's legs. If people did not like them they were pelted with mud and rotten food.

The only holidays were holy days such as Christmas and Easter and days of celebration such as Maytime and Harvest Supper. At these times there was dancing on the village green and a feast was set out on tables in the open air. Sometimes there were games such as skittles or blind man's buff. The peasants called it hoodman's blind.

Harvest supper in a medieval village

Some Things To Do

1. The oldest building in a village today is usually the church. You can often see interesting carvings and statues there. Look at the photographs on this page. Write a few words to say what each of these pictures show.

2. The pictures on page 23 were drawn about six hundred years ago. What birds and animals are shown? What tools did the peasants use? What clothes did they wear? Write a few words to say what you have found out by looking at these old pictures.

3. Draw pictures to show four of the jobs the peasants sometimes had to do for the lord of the manor. Write a few words underneath each picture to say what it shows.

Carvings in medieval churches

Afterwards

The life of the peasant slowly changed. In 1348 a terrible disease called the Black Death killed many people. Afterwards there were not so many peasants left to work on the land.

Many lords now thought it better to let the peasants pay rent in money for their strips of land. This was instead of making them do jobs of work without wages.

More and more peasants got their freedom and many peasants went to live in the towns where there was more work.

King John sealing the Magna Carta at Runnymede

6. MAGNA CARTA

Many people hated the way King John was ruling the country. He had raised taxes and fines to get money for himself and to pay for the war his soldiers were fighting in France. If people could not pay they were taken to prison.

At last the powerful barons decided to stop this. They drew up a document called the Grand Charter, or Magna Carta. In it they put down all the laws which would help the people and would stop the king from doing what he liked.

King John did not want to agree to this. He did not want to give up the freedom to rule as he liked. But the barons captured London and threatened to go to war if he did not put his seal to the agreement.

So on 15 June 1215 the king and the great lords of the land went to Runnymede, near Windsor Castle. The Charter was presented to John. A piece of wax was heated and put on the Charter. John pressed his seal to it. This was one of the most important days in English history because every freeman now had rights and laws to live by.

Some Things To Do

1. The picture on this page shows you what King John's seal looked like. Make your own seal by pressing a coin into plasticine.

2. Write out these sentences filling in the gaps with the best words you can think of:
Magna C . . . . . . simply means G . . . . . . C . . . . . . It was s . . . . . . by King . . . . . . on 15 June . . . . . . at R . . . . . . The rights of the b . . . . . . and of the f . . . . . . were written down in a long list.

3. Look at the picture opposite. Paint your own picture to show the barons' tents, their armour, the flags, the soldiers and the horses.

Afterwards

Fifty years later the first Parliament met at Westminster Hall in London. The barons made King Henry III (John's son) agree to a meeting with the bishops and the barons (the lords) and also with some of the common people. They were called the "commons".

King John's seal

Later they met in a special meeting place called the House of Commons. The barons and the bishops met in the House of Lords.

7. ENGLAND AT WAR WITH WALES AND SCOTLAND

King Edward presenting his son to the Welsh in April 1284

The crowd cheered as the King came to the gates of the castle at Caernarvon in North Wales. He had his newly-born son in his arms. In a strong voice he cried out: "He who has been born among you shall be your prince." According to legend this is what happened in April 1284. The King was Edward I. Edward had been fighting a war against soldiers from Wales who had supported Prince Llywelyn. Llywelyn had refused to do homage to Edward. This meant that he would not say that Edward was his lord. Now Llywelyn had been killed and Wales was joined to England.

Edward intended to make sure there were no more rebellions against his rule. He built a number of very strong castles in North Wales to make sure the Welsh people obeyed his laws.

Edward also fought in Scotland. He had taken the Scottish King prisoner and his soldiers had taken the Stone of Scone and placed it under the coronation chair in Westminster Abbey in London. The Kings of Scotland had always been crowned on the Stone of Scone.

In 1314 soldiers commanded by Robert Bruce of Scotland faced a very large English army by the banks of the Bannock Burn, a stream just outside Stirling in Scotland. Someone who was at the battle said the English "nobles and others fell into the Bannock Burn with their horses in the crush". The Scots had won.

Some Things To Do

1. Why did Edward I build strong castles in Wales?

2. Where was Edward's son born? Who is the present Prince of Wales?

3. Why do you think Edward's soldiers moved the Coronation Stone from Scone Abbey to Westminster Abbey? Why did this annoy the Scots?

4. Draw your own picture to show the battle of Bannockburn.

Afterwards

Scotland did not become joined to England until 1603. In that year a Scottish King (James VI) came to the throne as King James I of England.

The Battle of Bannockburn, 1314

8. THE PEASANTS' REVOLT

It was 1381. The people of London were worried and frightened. Peasants from Essex and Kent were marching on the city. They had already captured many towns. Later they killed the Archbishop of Canterbury.

The peasants were very angry about a new tax they had been asked to pay. They wanted their freedom from the lords of the manor. They elected a man called Wat Tyler to speak for them.

When they got to London the peasants demanded to speak to King Richard II. Richard was a boy of 15 but he rode to a place called Smithfield to speak to Wat Tyler. He agreed to everything the rebel peasants wanted although he knew he could not keep his promise. During their talk there was shouting and a scuffle. Wat Tyler was killed. The peasants were furious. They raised their bows and arrows. One writer said that Richard then rode towards the crowd and put his hand up in the air.
"Will you shoot your King?" he asked. "I will be your leader and give you what you want."

While he talked, the Mayor of London called up soldiers and so the meeting with the peasants ended.

The meeting between Wat Tyler and Richard II

Some Things To Do

1. What were the complaints of the peasants?

2. How many years ago is it since the Peasants' Revolt?

3. Draw a number of pictures to tell the story of Richard II and Wat Tyler. Write a few words under each picture to say what it shows.

Afterwards

After the Peasants' Revolt some of the leaders of the peasants were hanged. But the tax they hated was taken away. In the next hundred years almost all of the peasants were able to pay rent for their land. They no longer had to do jobs of work for the lord of the manor.

In some places there were only a few peasants left to work on the land. Some lords of the manor began to rear a lot of sheep. Wool was now one of the most important things produced on the farms of Britain in the Middle Ages.

9. LIFE IN A MEDIEVAL TOWN

A busy town in medieval times

Although it was still early in the morning the narrow street was noisy. The shopkeepers were putting their goods out on the counters. Their shops opened straight on to the street.

A schoolboy walking quickly to school tried to keep his feet clean but the street was filthy. There was a drain in the middle of the street filled with rubbish. Rotten food lying among piles of horse manure made the street stink.

One or two squeaking pigs ran through the street chased by a stray dog.

From time to time heavy carts, piled high with vegetables and fruit from the country, rattled by. Already shopkeepers were shouting to try to make people buy their goods. "Who will buy my pies?" cried one. "Here is the best cloth in the street!" cried another.

The houses in the street were made of wood and were very close to each other. If one house caught fire the flames quickly spread to the others. Each family living in the street had to have a bucket of water always handy. They also had a long pole with a hook on the end. This was to pull burning thatch down from the roof. Some houses were made of brick or stone but most were still made of wood. The upstairs floor in each house was built so that it stuck out over the street.

Medieval houses

Shops in medieval times

Some shops sold pies and roast meats. Others sold clothes, jewellery, tools, fresh fruit and vegetables, bread and many other things. Signs hung outside the shops to show what they sold. Most of the goods were made in a room behind the shop.

There were bakeries with ovens for making bread, pies and pastry. There were sheds where workpeople spun sheep's wool and where weavers made cloth.

These workshops only had one or two people working there. They were not like modern factories.

The shopkeepers and the merchants usually belonged to a guild. The members of a guild made rules about what their members could sell. Thev were

like a trade union. They helped their members if they were ill or in need of money. Some of the guilds built special guildhalls for their meetings, many of which can be seen today.

In those days only a few children went to school. Most stayed at home. When they were older they got jobs. Some became apprentices.

The apprentices spent five years or more learning a trade. They might be apprenticed to a baker, a butcher, a blacksmith or any one of a number of other trades.

Some apprentices worked hard. Others played football in the streets and spent their time in idleness. People in the towns often complained about the apprentices.

Some of the busiest towns in those days were ports. Ships from foreign lands brought spices, wines and many other goods into the harbours of the towns.

Merchants from other parts of Britain travelled to the ports, hoping to do business with the foreigners. Goods such as wool, cloth and corn were brought into town by horse and cart or by pack horse. A trader would have a long line of pack horses, each one laden with goods. Before the trader could enter the town he had to pay a sum of money, called a toll. After paying it he was allowed to go through the town gates.

In those days most towns were surrounded by high, thick walls. At night no-one was allowed to enter after the gates were shut.

A busy port in medieval times

A medieval town at night

There were many beggars in the towns. Some were peasants who had run away from the lord of the manor. At night time the streets were dark and gloomy. There were no proper street lights although sometimes lanterns were hung outside the houses.

It was dangerous to go on the streets after dark. Robbers and murderers found it easy to hide in the narrow streets waiting for a lonely stranger. There were no policemen. Instead a watchman came by from time to time.

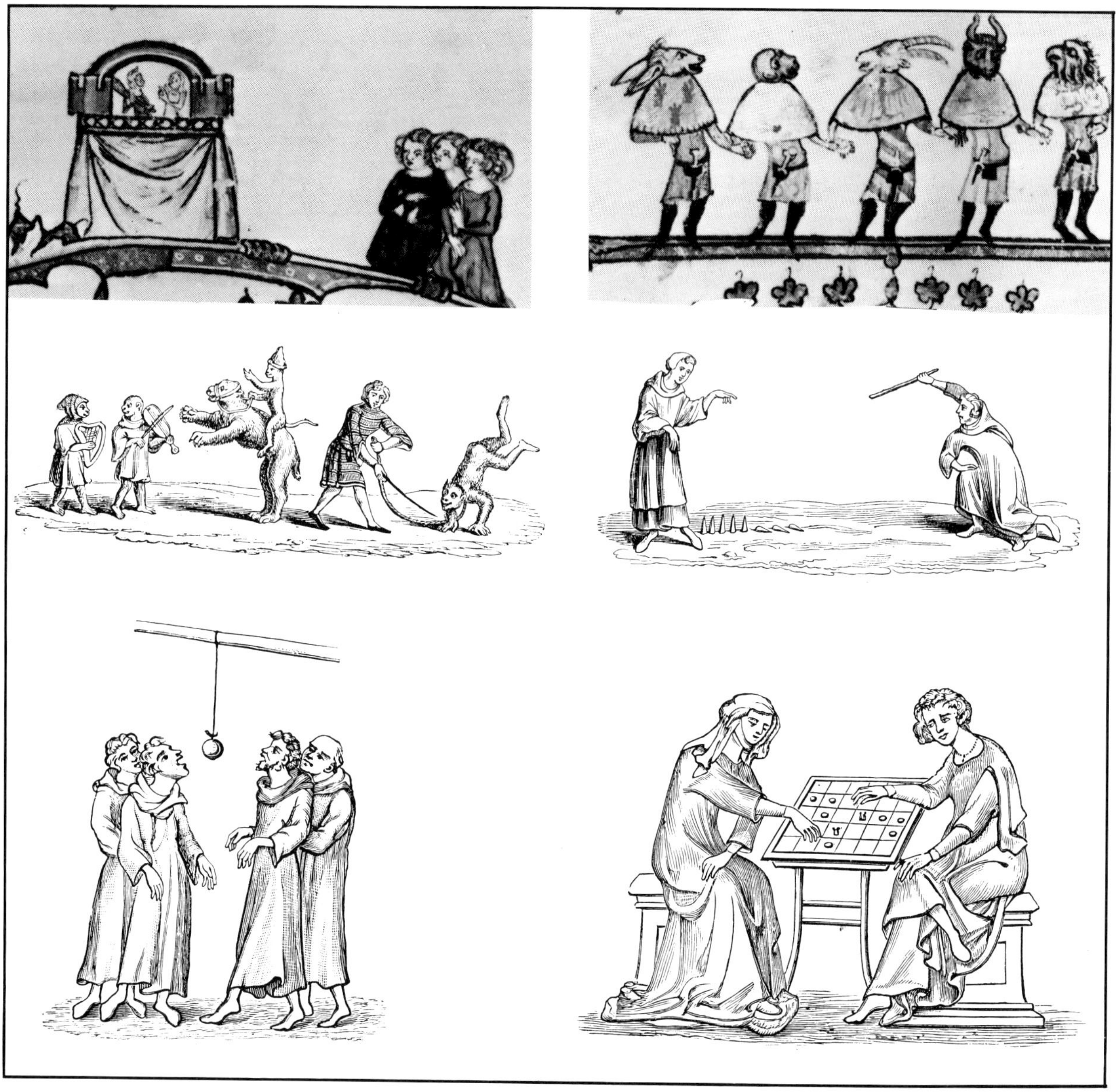

Games and amusements in medieval times

Pictures like these show us the games and musical instruments that were played in those days. In the top picture you can see a Punch and Judy show watched by three children. It looks very much like the Punch and Judy show you might see today.

One of these pictures shows a group of people called mummers. They were actors who put on fancy dress. Sometimes they put masks over their faces. They acted plays and made music.

You will probably be able to recognise some of the other games and entertainments shown in these pictures even though they were drawn about six hundred years ago.

Some Things To Do

1. Look at the games and entertainments shown in the pictures on these pages. Are they still popular today? Copy the pictures and write a few words underneath each picture to say what you think it shows.

2. Medieval towns often had terrible fires and outbreaks of diseases. Write down some of the things which caused these fires and diseases.

3. Look at the picture on pages 34–35. It shows a street in medieval times. Using the picture and text to help you, write an account of a day in the life of an apprentice.

Afterwards

London was the only large town in Britain in those times. People in London thought the streets were too busy. They did not like the noise of the traffic. Some complained about the smoke from coal fires. But the centre of London was still very close to the countryside.

Most of the other towns in Britain were quite small then. As the towns grew bigger new houses sometimes had to be built in fields outside the town walls. New churches also had to be built.

10. A HUNDRED YEARS OF WAR

It was 26 August 1346 at a place called Crecy in France. The French soldiers rushed forward eagerly seeking an easy victory. Their army was over twice as large as the English army. When the English archers could see the faces of their enemy they drew back their longbows and fired. A huge number of arrows flew towards the French soldiers. The air "snowed with arrows", as someone said afterwards.

Then there were three loud bangs. The English had fired three guns. This was the first time guns had ever been used in a battle. Some of the French soldiers were scared and ran back. They got in the way of horsemen who were charging forward. Hundreds of French lords and knights were killed. The English had won a great victory.

One of their heroes was the King's son, a young man who was later known as the Black Prince because he wore black armour.

The Battle of Crecy

Joan of Arc leading her army to victory at Orleans

About seventy years later on 25 October 1415, the English faced the French again, at Agincourt. Once again the French army was very much larger than that of the English.

Heavy rain had made the ground muddy. The French knights kept slipping in the mud as the English archers fired hundreds of arrows at them. It is said the French lost 7000 soldiers but the English only 100 men. The English now held a large part of France.

Several years later, a young French peasant girl called Joan of Arc said she had heard voices from God. The voices had told her to take an army and help the King to drive the English out of France.

She went to a knight called Robert, and asked him to give her some soldiers. He laughed at Joan and told her to go away. But Joan would not give up.

By now some people believed Joan really had come to save France. She was sent for by the King. She said, "I have been sent by God. Give me some soldiers and I will drive the English back to their own country."

At last Joan did lead the French soldiers in battle. At the head of her troops, and dressed in white armour, she drove the English away from the town of Orleans. Later, people called her the Maid of Orleans because she had saved the town from defeat.

Siege of Rouen

Joan of Arc being burnt at the stake

But Joan had many enemies as well as friends. Priests did not like the way she said she had heard voices from God. The English soldiers feared her and thought she must be a witch. She was captured by the English and put on trial for witchcraft. She was found guilty and burned at the stake.

She was only 19 years old.

Some Things To Do

1. The picture below was drawn at about the time of the battle of Crecy. Write down what you think it shows. Why do you think the English soldiers were very good archers?

2. Look at the bottom picture on the opposite page. It was drawn about the time of the battle of Agincourt. It shows English soldiers surrounding a French town. Draw your own picture of this siege. Write a few words underneath to say what your picture shows.

3. Write out these sentences filling in the gaps with the best words you can think of.
Joan of ...... came from ......
She said she had heard ......
They had told her ...... She led the French soldiers in battle wearing ...... After she saved Orleans she was called ...... She was only 19 years of age when she was ......

Afterwards

About twenty years after the death of Joan of Arc, the French finally drove the English out of France. By 1453 Calais was the only French town still held by English soldiers.

A hundred years of war had come to an end.

Joan of Arc was the heroine of France. In 1920, nearly 500 years later, she was made a saint.

Shooting at the butts

11. THE WARS OF THE ROSES

The Princes in the Tower

For thirty years there had been civil war while two great families fought for the throne of England. On one side was the Yorkists, whose emblem was a white rose. On the other side was the family of Lancaster. Their emblem was a red rose.

Edward V was from the house of York, but in 1483 he was only 12 years old. He and his brother were put in the Tower of London, for safety, by their Uncle Richard. Then Richard became the new king of England, Richard III. During the summer the two little princes were sometimes seen playing in the garden. Then they disappeared.

To this day no one knows for sure what happened. There is no doubt that the two princes were killed. Who the murderer was is still a mystery. Many people said it must have been Richard III. But no one can really be sure. Other people could have done this horrible murder.

Some Things To Do

1. What colour rose would you have given to Richard III?

2. Look at the picture below showing a battle during the Wars of the Roses. What weapons and armour did the soldiers carry? Draw your own picture of this battle. Write a few words underneath saying what your picture shows.

Afterwards

In 1485 King Richard III was defeated and killed at the battle of Bosworth near Leicester.

King Henry VII, who took the throne from him, began the reign of the Tudor kings and queens.

A battle in the Wars of the Roses

MORE EXERCISES

William the Conqueror

1. What weapons were used at the battle of Hastings?

2. Which army fought with battleaxes?

3. What is the Bayeux Tapestry? Write a few sentences to describe two pictures from the Bayeux Tapestry.

4. How did William the Conqueror show the people of London how powerful he was?

5. Who rebelled against William after the battle of Hastings?

Living in a Castle

1. Write a few words to say what each of these was: portcullis, drawbridge, moat, battering ram.

2. Write a few sentences to say how enemy soldiers tried to capture a castle.

3. What was a tournament?

4. Where in the castle did the baron's children play?

The Murder of Thomas Becket

1. Why did pilgrims travel to Canterbury Cathedral after the death of Becket?

2. Write a few words to describe Henry II.

3. Why do you think the monks and priests were frightened when they saw the four knights?

4. Do you think Thomas Becket could have saved himself from being murdered by the four knights?

A Knight at the Crusades

1. Who were the Saracens? Who was their leader at the time of the Crusades?

2. Why was Richard given the name of the Lionheart?

3. How did the Duke of Austria get his own back on Richard?

4. Write down the names of three things which came to Britain as a result of the Crusades.

Life in a Medieval Village

1. Write a few sentences to describe a peasant's hut in a medieval village.

2. What did the farmers grow in the three large fields surrounding the village?

3. How did the peasants pay the lord of the manor for the strips of land they farmed?

4. What things about life in a medieval village would you have hated?

Magna Carta

1. What was the name of the place where King John agreed to put his seal on Magna Carta?

2. What was Magna Carta? What does the name mean in English?

3. Why did the barons make John agree to Magna Carta?

England at War with Wales and Scotland

1. Why did Edward I call his son the Prince of Wales?

2. Write down the names of two Welsh or Scottish leaders who fought against the English at this time.

3. Where did the Scottish army defeat the English in battle in 1314?

The Peasants' Revolt

1. Why did the peasants rebel against the government during the reign of King Richard II?

2. Who was Wat Tyler?

3. What happened to the peasants after the rebellion failed?

Life in a Medieval Town

1. Write a description of a street in a medieval town.

2. Why were the streets filthy?

3. How did people try to put out a fire in a medieval town?

4. Write a few sentences to describe the picture of a medieval port.

5. Why was it dangerous to walk outside after dark in a medieval town?

6. Write down the names of five games or entertainments which were popular in medieval times.

A Hundred Years of War

1. What weapon helped the English to beat the French at the battles of Crecy and at Agincourt?

2. Who was Joan of Arc? Write a few sentences to describe her life.

3. Why did the English think Joan was a witch?

4. Why was Joan called the Maid of Orleans?

The Wars of the Roses

1. Who were the Princes in the Tower?

2. What is a civil war?

3. Why was the war between the Yorkists and the Lancastrians called the Wars of the Roses?

4. Who became king after the death of Richard III?

INDEX